Published By Robert Corbin

@ Stan Frisbie

The Art of Dog Training: Effective Training Techniques

for Your Hyperactive and Easily Distracted Dog

Nurturing a Strong Bond and Good Behavior with

Your Canine

ISBN 978-87-94477-08-6

AF353880

TABLE OF CONTENTS

Chapter 1

A Dog's Life Stages

If you haven't owned a puppy before, you may notice that a puppy is quite different compared to dogs in their adulthood. However, you may find that some dogs in their adolescence still act like a two-month-old puppy. In order to make sure you are taking care of your dog in the most effective way, you must get an understanding of what each different life stage brings and what things are needed to change. In this chapter, we will be discussing the differences and traits of the three stages of a dog's life; puppyhood, adulthood, and seniorhood.

Puppyhood

Adulthood/adolescence

Senior hood

Hip dysplasia: This condition makes it hard for your dog to walk or run. Medication or surgery are possible solutions depending on how severe the condition is.

Orthopedic problems: This a condition due to normal wear and tear in the bones and joints of your dog. Arthritis is common for dogs at this stage in life.

Hypothyroidism: This condition slows your dog down and often leads to obesity or heart problems. Make sure to take your senior dog to frequent check-ups as this can be detected with a simple blood test and is easily managed using medication.

Eye problems: Conditions like cataracts and hamper vision occur in older dogs and can lead to blindness.

Cancer: Cancer is a common disease that can show up in all phases of a dog's life but is most commonly found in older dogs.

Chapter 2

Basic Commands In Dog Training

Name recognition training

Sit and stay command training

Down and stay command training

Place command training

Go command training

Come back command training

Don't correct your dog when it is coming towards you because he is doing something desirable.

Punishing him or correcting him midway before he gets to you might get him confused, and he may lose trust in you.

The come-back or recall training exercise should be made as much fun for your dog as possible

Give your dog full attention when you call him to come towards you. Ensure you have a long line attached to your dog's collar to guide him when the need arises.

Chasing your dog isn't the best idea and not part of the ideal training. This will eventually lead to a 'chase-me' game, and humans most often lose at the end of the day.

Practice the 'come back' cues at least 8-10 times daily throughout the life of your dog

Ensure you don't call your dog to come back for something he may find fearful or unpleasant. For instance, calling your dog again from playing and immediately putting the leash on him and restricting his movement might not be too pleasant for the dog.

Always give your dog a treat worthwhile and fabulous that it just couldn't help but come back to you anytime you call for it.

Rather than punish your dog for failure to come to you after calling it, try running backward away from your dog and let him chase you, squeak one of his favorite toys, whistle, or show him food.

Teaching the Basic 'Come-Back' behavior

Locate a quiet place with little or no distractions

Get your clicker, treats and dog ready for the training

Put a treat on the floor and allow the dog to go for it. Walk away from your dog and call its name while holding out a visible treat for it. If you get the attention of your dog, immediately use the word 'come' or 'come-back' in a happy tone.

Use the clicker once the dog begins to walk towards you. Verbally praise your dog as it comes to you and gives it a treat while touching its collar when it eventually gets to you. (This is essential because sometimes, your dog may decide to play a smart one on you, grab the treat and run).

The above steps should be practiced for about 8 – 10 times before taking a break.

The drop-it command training

Drop-it training:

Get your treats such as cheese or dried liver, clicker, and dog ready for this training

With a treat in your hand, encourage your dog to chew on one of his favorite toys or food.

Once she has the object in her mouth, put a piece of treat (most likely food) close to his nose and use the cue 'drop-it.'

Click when he drops the toy in her mouth and feed your dog with the food you brought close to her nose while picking up the item dropped from his mouth. After this, you can return the item to him.

Encourage your dog to pick up the object as you continually practice the training. However, you must be cautious because once your dog becomes aware that it will get a treat, he will most likely not pick up the item again and keep his mouth free to receive more treats.

Keep your treats in handy and practice this training whenever you see your dog randomly pick an item or toy.

At least ten repetitions a day is advised.

Sometimes though, you shouldn't give back the object to your dog if it is a dangerous object or restricted from the dog's use. However, ensure you give your dog an extra sweet treat if you aren't given the object back to your dog.

If your dog becomes fully conversant with the training, you can bring your hands close to your dog's nose without actually holding the treat. The chances are that your dog will drop whatsoever it is holding. If this is the case, click and give your dog a treat out of your pocket.

If possible, give her an extra treat at least an equivalent of three ordinary treats the first time you use the empty finger approach.

After your dog has mastered this training, you can spice things up with a tasty item, which could be a carrot.

Hold the treat on the one hand and offer the other side of the item to your dog and encourage it to chew it while still holding it in your hand and then give your dog the drop its cues.

Again give your dog the equivalent of three treats if he gets the command correctly the first time

Following consistent training of your dog, you can start training your dog with real-life objects around him such as pens, shoes, clothes e.t.c. Once this is successful, you can begin practicing the drop it cues whenever you are outside with your dog

Rules to observe in the drop-it training

If you have a dog that enjoys playing the grab and chase game, then you have to teach him that you aren't going to chase him when he grabs the item. The best move is to ignore your dog, and he will most definitely drop the object when he gets tired of it. You can also try distracting him, thereby dropping the object unknowingly.

Trust me, sometimes even the yummiest treat cannot make your dog drop what the dangerous item it is holding, or you probably don't have the time and patience to let it drop it then you should place your fingers on her jaw, locate the canines, push in and pull up. This move will open your dog's mouth, and you can retrieve the item. After successfully removing the item, give your dog a treat and ensure you subsequently keep such an item out of reach of your dog.

Ensure your practice drop it whenever you play a tug and fetch game with your dog.

If your dog has a valuable item in his mouth, try to bribe him by showing him a treat but ensure it doesn't become a habit.

House training/potty training

Listening training for your dog

Dog Training for Barking

Training a barking dog seeking attention

Training a barking dog hearing or seeing
something interesting

Training a barking dog as a result of fear and
aggression

Training a barking dog who is bored

The Three Noble Truth of Dog Training

Timing: The importance of timing in your training cannot be overemphasized. Scientifically, a dog has about 1.3 seconds to associate a cause with an effect. This further validates the saying that 'you have to catch them in the act.' Generally, dogs believe it is being corrected, or rewarded for its current action or behavior. In essence, dogs (including puppies) live in the present, completely neglecting what happens aftermath. Timing thus has a significant implication on the success of your training. What this implies is that you have to monitor your dog carefully to discover its mistakes or desired behavior exhibited when exactly they occur. This will help you either reward them or correct them almost immediately. Delaying for more than 1.3 seconds after such action or behavior has been exhibited may confuse the dog due to the lag in time of communication. The dog would not know precisely what it is being rewarded or corrected for when the timing is wrong. Timing is essential despite the training method you want to employ. Without efficient timing, your training would most likely not yield expected positive results.

Motivation: Positive encouragement promotes and encourages desirable behavior from your dog. Conversely, negative feedback or response from you makes your dog quit its undesirable behavior. Rewards and treats are often given to your dog as a mark of encouragement during training to continue the desired behavior. Following such reward and treats, the dog would most likely exhibit such positive behavior more often. Similarly, corrections that may include verbal, physical, sound, or leash when the dog makes mistakes or exhibit behaviors that are unwanted will make such behavior less likely to occur in the future.

Consistency: In training your dog either by behavioral modification or brain training or obedience training, in fact, whatsoever training you met out to your dog, consistency is critical. You simply cannot afford any gray area or lapses in your dog training. The training process and method must be distinct; a rule is a rule! No bending of the rules and procedures. For instance, if you want your dog to quit chewing your items and furniture, then you have to consistently reinforce and inculcate such training aimed at eliminating such undesired behavior. Regardless of your mood, whether happy or sad, your rules for your dog training should be set out and followed. Just because you got a promotion at work and you are happy doesn't mean you should allow your dog bite and chew on your trousers or shoes when you return. Alright, lets for a brief moment assume you let your dog bite and chew your trousers on shoes, and you fail to reinforce the principle you had already laid out just because you are happy. What happens when a colleague offends you at work the following day, and you come home angry and decide to vent some anger towards your dog by effecting the principle of 'no biting and chewing your stuff'? Of course, the dog would be as confused as confused gets. Should it bite or not? At that moment, it is caught at a crossroads between two decisions as a result of your inconsistency in training. In essence, you must be black and white with your rules, remaining 100% consistent. Making use of these three noble truths results in a dog that trusts and feels entirely safe with you set out rules and training processes.

Chapter 3

Understanding Doggy Language

The Key to Reading Your Dog's Body Language

Posture

Tail

Face

Barking

Growling

Whining

Whimpering

Howling

Chapter 4

Taking Care Of Your Dog

Essential Care for Your New German

Feeding

Dry food

Wet food

Raw food

How Much to Feed your German

5 lbs: half cup to three-quarters cup

10 lbs: three-quarters cup to one cup

20 lbs: one and a quarter cups to one and three-quarters cups

40 lbs: two and a quarter cups to three cups

60 lbs: three to four cups

80 lbs: three and two-third cups to five cups

100 lbs: four and a quarter cups to six cups

When to Feed Fido

Switching foods

Day 1-2 Mix ¼ new with ¾ old foods

Day 2-4 Mix ½ new with ½ old

Day 5-6 Mix ¾ new with ¼ old

Day 7 100% of the new dog food

Healthy Treats and Snacks

Oatmeal

Yogurt

Apples with the seeds removed

Peanut butter

Cheese

Bananas

Beef jerky or other jerkies

Meat, cooked or raw after being properly frozen

Berries

Melons

Green beans. Be careful, as this can act as a laxative for your dog.

Peas

Squash and pumpkin

Brewer's yeast. Not baker's yeast, which can make your dog very sick.

Carrots

Eggs

Salmon or other fish

Foods to Avoid at all Costs

Table scraps

Onion or garlic

Chocolate. Especially dark chocolate

Grapes or raisins

Macadamia nuts

Fruit pits or seeds

Soft bones such as from pork or poultry

Potato peelings or green potatoes

Rhubarb leaves

Yeast dough or baker's yeast

Human vitamins or medications

Broccoli

Caffeine

Alcohol

Mushrooms

Persimmons

Avocadoes

Raw egg. Can give your dog salmonella poisoning

Xylitol which can be found in foods such as brand-named peanut butters

Exercising your german

Brushing

Bathing

Lay down the slip-resistant mat nearby your tub for safety and comfortability

Now gently ease your German into the bathtub. Dogs usually resist baths until they are used to the process. Be sure to make him feel relaxed by offering lots of praise and a treat.

Once your German Shepherd is in the bathtub, you can start running the water. Before soaking your dog, test the water temperature with your fingers carefully. Make sure that it is comfortable, lukewarm water.

Get your dog's entire body wet and begin rubbing in the shampoo to create a gentle lather. Don't use so much that you can't rinse it all out, but also don't use so little that you can't create a rich lather. Try your best to avoid his eyes and mouth. Rinse face often as necessary during bathing.

Trick: Bathe his head last. This is the part that he will shake and get shampoo all over you, the floor, the walls, and well, you get the picture

Now rinse him thoroughly using lukewarm water. Gently work the shampoo out with your hands from top to bottom. Do this several times to get all of the shampoo out so his natural oils can get busy keeping him healthy

Now turn the water off and wrap him in a towel. Rub him down thoroughly. You can use a hair dryer after this to effectively dry his entire body. Caution: NEVER USE A HOT SETTING WHEN USING A BLOW DRYER! Place the setting on cool or warm and test it 6 inches from your bare skin on your inner side wrist. If you can hold it there indefinitely, your dog will feel comfortable while keeping him happy and from harm.

Nails

Hold your dog between your legs if he is small, or if larger, have him stand.

Pick up each foot with your empty hand, so it bends naturally and comfortably. Trim each dog nail separately and delicately, taking your time on each. You never want to hit his quick, which is inside the dog's nail which contains blood vessels and sensitive nerve endings. Focus on the furthest end from the paw, the most translucent part of his nail that you can see through when you hold a light to his paw.

Dogs with white nails will have *obvious quicks*, which are pink and darker and thicker than the rest of his nail. Germans can have white nails but are more likely to have black or a combination of black and white.

In *black nails* that you can't see the quick, trim little pieces of the horn of his nail. Then inspect the nail to see if there is bleeding. Do it a bit at a time and be patient. You never want to hit the quick or you will cause your German Shepherd pain and as a result, a bad association with nail trimming.

File the end to a smooth, round surface with a regular emery board.

Consider a smoothing oil, like coconut oil, to soften his paws. Use beeswax to heal cracks.

Your german's teeth

Put a dab on your finger and let him smell it and lick it to get him comfortable.

Then try inserting your finger into his mouth and rubbing his gums gently and without too much force.

Soon he'll get used to this without too much resistance. When he lets you do this without freaking out, you can try using the dog tooth brush.

Use gentle but firm strokes to get his gums and all of his teeth. It won't be perfect, but the idea is to get most of his dental surface area covered in the foam of the toothpaste.

There is no need to rinse. He will swallow the toothpaste without problems. However, try to encourage him to drink from his water bowl after a brushing.

Eyes

Anal sacs

Ready to Expunge? Here's How:

Don a pair of plastic or rubber gloves.

Put your dog in a bathtub. This can get messy.

Rub gently upward and inward, pressing the glands toward his anus. Like a teenager's zit on prom nite.

The fluid should ooze out of his anus. It should be brown and strong-smelling oil. If nothing comes out, you may want to take him to the vet to have them emptied.

Shots for your German Shepherd

Health problems

Mentally Stimulating Activities for your German

Retrieval games. Add challenges by hiding toys or throwing them into hard-to-access places so that your dog must puzzle out how to get the toy.

Obstacle courses. Turn your home, garage, or back yard into an obstacle course and make your dog overcome it by rewarding dog treats when accomplishing completion.

A Kong full of peanut butter. He can spend hours trying to lick the peanut butter out. An occupied dog means a dog who isn't getting into trouble.

Flyball. This will keep him active physically and mentally.

Socialization and play with other dogs. He will invent his own games and feel very stimulated in the company of other dogs. Take your German Shepherd to the dog park or enroll him in puppy classes where he can play with other dogs.

Herding livestock or Triebball. Triebball uses balls that mimic herd animals that dogs must manage.

Tracking. Hide an object in the woods or a field and let your dog find it with his natural scent abilities.

Herding trials or tests. These will let your German use his natural herding ability.

Agility games. Set up an agility course in your yard and teach your dog obedience and tricks as you teach him to navigate the equipment.

Chapter 5

Train Your Dog Simple Basic Rules

Simple Rules for Dog Training

Galion:

Concentrate on the conduct you need.

Use power free strategies.

Fortify great conduct.

Set up preparing for progress.

Show your pooch discretion.

Chapter 6

Health Care Basics For The Dog

Nutrition

Kibble is a 100% dry food and the one that is most commonly used. It is the most economical and offers a complete and balanced diet for dogs that come in all sizes and different ages. This is recommended for adult dogs to help maintain the health of their teeth and digestion.

Canned food is a wet food that is the most expensive type of food to feed your dog. However, dogs find this to be the tastiest. This type of food may be good for puppies that have not developed the teeth or digestion strong enough yet or senior dogs that may have weaker teeth and digestion. If it's not a case of need, most owners reserve canned food as a treat as it is the most expensive type of food.

Semi-moist food usually comes in single-serving packets. This is not a common type of food as it is not very economical and serves little purpose. A lot of the time people use this as a treat for their dog.

Hygiene

Bathing your puppy

So, how exactly do you wash your dog properly? This is important to learn so you don't go into the situation unprepared. Having a well-trained dog is important for this task as it is easiest when they are calm and sitting still. If your dog is not trained well, you may want to put them through behavioral training before taking on a task like this, especially if you have a dog of a large breed. Here are a few tips on how to bathe your pup properly:

Brush your dog's hair/fur before the bath. Make sure your dog doesn't have any matted hair as it tends to hold lots of water. Washing your dog with matted hair will cause skin irritation. If you aren't able to brush or cut out those mats by yourself, it is recommended to take them to a professional groomer to have it done. Do not attempt to brush or cut out any mats if you aren't confident. Before you start the bath, you can put a large cotton ball in your dog's ear to help keep out water. This will prevent ear infections or irritations.

Use lukewarm water to bathe your dog. Although humans typically shower with hot water, your dog's skin is different from ours. The water you use should not be hotter than what you would use to wash a baby. Make sure that the water is not hot to touch but is a comfortable warmth. For larger breeds, keep the water even cooler as they overheat easily.

Talk to your pet calmly during the bath. For dogs that are feisty during bath time, try to soothe them by talking to them gently. Don't yell, shout, or panic during this time as they may misunderstand the situation as being intimidating. After a few baths they will learn that you are not trying to harm them and it can be quite an enjoyable experience.

Use dog shampoo when bathing your dog. Dog shampoo dries out skin less than what human shampoo would. Lather the shampoo gently into your dog's body and massage it all over. Be careful not to get any shampoo in their eyes as it is extremely irritating.

Rinse well. Make sure you are rinsing your dog until there are no more soap suds on its body. Any shampoo left on your dog's body after the bath can irritate its skin.

Air dry your dog after the bath. Avoid using blow dryers to dry your dog's fur. Blow dryers tend to be too hot for a dog's skin. If needed, there are blow-dryers that are designed for dogs that you can purchase. These blow dryers expel air in lower temperatures that won't cause irritation.

Reward your dog after the bath. Follow up the bath with lots of praise, petting, play, or treats. This will help your dog associate bath time to a reward which will make them less irritable during the process. A lot of the times your dog may be frustrated after the bath so encouraging exercise afterward can help your dog blow off some steam.

Brushing your dog's teeth

Cleaning your puppy's bed

Routine visits help veterinarians assess how your dog is progressing through life and may help discover any underlying health conditions that your pet may have. A lot of the times our dogs can have a serious issue that we aren't able to notice but a veterinarian would be able to pick these things up. The earlier you spot a problem, the easier it is to correct it or at least slow the condition down.

During a general check-up, the veterinarian will perform a physical examination. This usually consists of a check that starts from your dog's nose all the way to their tail. They will inspect everything from the mouth, coat, paws, skin, and the tail. Checking your dog's dental health is an important part of the check-up as 80% of dogs are afflicted with dental problems.

Bringing your dog to regular general check-ups will allow your veterinarian to make sure that your pup is caught up on his/her vaccines.

Vaccinations are extremely important because they protect your dog against diseases that are fatal. Moreover, it also keeps other animals around you and your pup safe as well.

Chapter 7

Working on your Puppy's Daily Routines

Sadly, all play and no work makes Sparky a raucous pet.Just like individuals, canines likewise need to follow an everyday daily practice to make them more reasonable. During the initial not many long stretches of his visit, there are a few things that you should do to guarantee that your canine will remain fit and polite. This will take a ton of difficult work, however it will pay off in the long term.

Factors to Consider when Creating a Schedule for your Pooch

There is no strong response with regards to making the best everyday daily schedule for your pet. In any case, you really want to consider these few factors:

1. Feeding Time

Compared to grown-up canines, pups should be taken care of all the more regularly so they will grow up sound and blissful. You want to take care of them something like three adjusted dinners daily, which is very like humans.

Scheduling your pet 's taking care of time is really more straightforward than it looks since you can design it around your own supper plan. Preferably, you should take care of your pet at around 7 am, 12 pm and 5 pm.

Follow this taking care of timetable for no less than three to four months.

2. Potty Schedule

 You can without much of a stretch decide your canine's potty timetable on the off chance that he follows a customary taking care of routine.

As a guideline, little dogs need to go potty 3 to 4 hours consistently. That is on the grounds that canines find it difficult to control themselves when they are youthful. On the off chance that you don't apportion some time for them, expect a major wreck in your residing room.

Likewise, you should likewise look for a decent spot where your little guy can do his business calmly. This will instruct him that he can go potty at a particular time and he can't just do it in all aspects of the house.

3. Learning the Right Keywords

In the field of canine preparation, watchwords are fundamental terms that you can use to provide an order or let your canine know if his activities are positive or not. Instances of these words are"no" and"good."

To assist your puppy with remembering the catchphrases quicker, ensure that you just utilize basic terms that have not many syllables. Furthermore, ensure that you are steady with these terms. Your puppy needs to hear similar words a few times to relate these with the right meaning.

4. Playtime

Even assuming you are occupied with your pet's acquiescence preparing and your own everyday timetable, ensure that you actually dispense essentially a couple of long periods of recess with your fuzzy buddy. Proactive tasks can make your dog solid and it will likewise reinforce your bond with him.

If you have any desire to begin your little guy's morning with a work-out daily practice, it is ideal to do it before he takes his first dinner. Subsequently, you can take him for a short walk outside. The ideal routine is to work out, feed your dog, do holding exercises, feed your dog, thus on.

Chapter 8

Dog Training Shopping List

There are a couple of things that you have to buy in order to train a dog easily. These include:

Treats

These are the very first things you should keep in mind. You need dog biscuits or kibbles to be able to reward your dog each time he does something right. There are many different kinds and your puppy may not like some of them. Make sure to try several different types to see which one makes your puppy very happy. Also, keep in mind that some are healthier than other and each treat has a calorie count. You don't want to over do it, sometimes a "good boy" with a pat on the head is reward enough.

Clicker

A Clicker is also important because it creates the right atmosphere for training. Used with treats, it gives your puppy an audible single to understand that he should follow you.

Clicker training is important because:

It creates a rewarding atmosphere. When this happens, the dog is easily encouraged and motivated to try new things and improve himself.

The clicker makes it easy for dog to understand the concept of time. It helps him understand what you want him to know, when he's getting a reward, and why.

Training sessions become easier because of the said rewarding atmosphere. The dog will find the sessions to be exciting, and thus, he'll be able to learn more.

The puppy becomes more patient and willing to learn.

And most importantly, it strengthens the bond between you and your dog!

Food

Of course, a dog needs to eat, too. Check Chapter 7 for the right kinds of food that you should buy for your furry friend.

Grooming Tools

Bristle brushes. These are for breeds with short and straight-haired coats.

Pin Brushes. These are meant for breeds with long, double coats.

Rubber brushes. These are perfect for short-haired dogs.

Slicker Brushes. These are best for those with medium coats.

You should also buy combs, shedding tools, clippers, soap, shampoos, and conditioners, as well. Any soap or hair product you purchase, should be specially made for dogs and do not substitute it with human products.

Housetraining Items

Plastic Bags. Save those bags from the store! They come in handy, especially during times of potty emergencies. These can also be used to pick up dog poop.

Pet Stain Cleaner. This helps keep the bathroom or your puppy's potty place clean.

Leash. Nylon, cotton, or leather will do, and it should be around 6 feet long. This way, your puppy will not run around playing while trying to poop.

Fencing. This should be placed outside, and should serve as a boundary between your dog and other dogs outside.

Doggie sweater/jacket. These will come in handy during colder months for trips outside.

Doggie door. This is a good tool to consider if you have a secure fence outside and a safe place for your dog to roam. It's much easier to house train your puppy if he can go outside whenever he pleases.

Puppy Pads or Newspapers. These are essential, especially during the first few days of house training. Lay them across the floor in the same area. Sometimes your puppy won't be able to make it outside, but given time he will learn that the newspapers are an ok spot to relieve himself!

Crate/Kennel. Make sure it is big enough to hold your puppy both now and as he grows. He should not just fit, but also be able to lie, turn around, or sit in it.

Collar. A snap collar or flat buckle would not only keeps the puppy on a leash, it is also be a good place to put identification on.

Crate Training Items

1. Plastic Crates. They can be used every day, and are also essential for travel. If you're the kind of person who often wants to travel with his puppy, try this one.

2. Wicker Crate. Wicker Crates give the effect that the puppy is in a basket, just like a baby. However, they may not last a long time because the puppy might chew on it. Yikes!

3. Wire Crate. And of course, you have wire crates. They could be covered with blankets, and also provide great airflow—which is good for the puppy. You can also try putting dividers to separate feeding bowls from his bed space!

Beds

There are many different types of beds to consider, from expensive to cheap. Each one has its own pros and cons, consider this list before making a purchase.

Bolster Beds. Research shows that most puppies favor bolster beds because they're quite comfortable. Bolster beds are like padded beds, but provide additional support for the dogs, because they could rest their heads at elevated angles. The problem with bolster beds, is they're a bit pricier than other options. Bolster beds are also bulky—so make sure you do have a lot of space for them.

Cedar-filled Beds. Cedar-filled beds are also padded beds and can be bought from most pet stores. The difference between these beds and simple padded beds is the fact that cedar-filled beds are created to mask a pet's odor, especially in confined spaces. However, since the bed is trying to mask your pet's odor, the bed emits the smell of cedar—and the bed might be a problem if you are not comfortable with that smell. Dogs may also find the smell a bit annoying, and you'd see them roll around a little too much. Cedar filled beds are also said to be not as comfortable as cotton beds.

Simple Padded. Simple-padded beds are the most common kind of pet beds. They're basically just pillows covered with soft and comfortable materials, and are also stuffed, usually with cotton. They're the most affordable bed, making them a favorite of many pet owners. Choose simple padded beds that are easy to wash.

Orthopedic. Orthopedic beds are mostly used by old, arthritic dogs. But, if your puppy is suffering from hip dysplasia, or has recently survived an accident, orthopedic beds may help them sleep better. Orthopedic beds are designed in such a way that the dog's body will not touch the ground. This prevents pain in his back. Also the extra padding decrease the amount of cold air that your dog feels. This way, his condition would not worsen, and his joints can start recuperating. Of course, as you would expect, orthopedic beds are a bit expensive.

Cots. Cots are next in line to simple-padded beds, in terms of affordability and ease of use. Cots are lifted slightly above ground and could be placed outside, so that the puppy could have a place to rest outdoors, too. Cots are also recommended for dogs with thick coats because they provide proper air circulation to prevent your dog from getting too hot.

Corner. Since they're meant to fit in the corner of a room, corner beds are perfect for puppies, and small dog breeds, as well as for houses that are not very spacious. It is also quite comfortable, but is not recommended for older, bigger dogs.

Cave. Cave beds give some puppies a sense of security because they know they could hide in them. The beds are characterized by having a hood, which makes for easy snuggling. Cave beds are also perfect for colder seasons because they offer warmth to the dogs. They're a bit expensive, though, so you do have to be ready for that.

Heated and Cooled. Heated and Cooled beds are special kinds of beds that are meant for puppies who are experiencing medical problems. They could be used for cooling or heating, depending on the weather. This helps your dog easily adjust and sleep.

Nest. Nest beds are also quite comfortable. They are half-shaped boxes or circles with pillows resting in the bottom. Not only would the dog feel comfortable, he'd also feel safe because he could snuggle towards the bottom, and use the elevated part of the bed for sightseeing or playtime.

 Framed beds. If you have a lot of money to spare, you could try using framed beds. They add to the aesthetic quality of your house because they look like real beds with their mattresses on spring surface. Frames protect the beds from falling apart and there are many designs and styles to choose from.

Take some time to consider your budget and your puppies needs. They are going to spend a lot of time on their new bed and it's essential you spend some time considering which one it will be.

Now that you know what you need, it's time to start house training the dog!

CHAPTER 9

Dog Breed And Characteristics

This goes back to the previous chapter when I mentioned that you should do research regarding what characteristics each breed exhibit. This chapter will address some of the general behavioral attributes of the different dog breed types. These are not meant to be the ironclad rules of behavior, but just a generalization of what we've seen from different breeds. Like humans, all dogs are individuals and have their own personalities.

Protection dog type: Protection dogs were originally bred for herding other animals or acting as flock guards. We now use them for various different purposes, such as guarding homes and property, or for activities like Schutzhund (a

German terminology for "protection dog") sport. Protection dogs often exhibit confidence, dominance, and a high capability to interact and work with humans. However, protection dogs often display behaviors like dominant aggression, possessiveness, and separation anxiety.

Breeds of protection dogs include the following: German Sheperd, Akita, Rottweiler, Doberman pinscher, Great Dane, Boxer, Bull Mastiff and Mastiff

Herding dog type: Herding dogs retain more of a "wolf-like" behavior than any other dog type, with the exception of the Northern Breeds. This is due to their tendency to stalk and chase (herd) other animals on a regular basis. Herding breeds are generally used to herd sheep and cattle, but they can often be flock protectors as well. These dogs are usually medium sized, very sensitive and agile, and quick to use their teeth to guide their flock. They are also demanding, dominant, loyal, and highly obedient. However, herding breeds tend to display fear-based aggression, destructive tendencies, noisiness, and separation anxiety.

Breeds of herding dogs include the following: Border Collie, German Shepherd, Belgian Shepherd, Australian Shepherd, Kelpie, Sheepdog, Bearded Collie and Bouvier

Retriever dog type: Retrievers do what they are born to do – retrieve items, whether they're in water, on land, or in the air. Most retrievers are good natured, very outgoing, and quite energetic. People have bred these dogs specifically for a wolf's prey drive – bringing back the prey to the den. In addition, retrievers can be submissive, which is very useful if you want them to give up their possessions to the owners. Retrievers are typically energetic, happy at almost all times, dominant, vocal, very obedient, ball/frisbee oriented, and has a tremendous ability to interact and work with humans. However, they also display typical problems, such as destructiveness, separation anxiety, noisiness, and hyperactive tendencies.

Breeds of retriever dogs include the following: Golden retriever, Flat Coated Retriever, Curly Coated Retriever, Labrador Retrievers, and Chesapeake Bay Retrievers

Spaniel dog type: The word "Spaniel" actually comes from Spain. And indeed, some of the group of dogs did come from that country. Spaniels are primarily used as hunting dogs. They are bred to flush or spring animals from the bushes, so that the hunter will be able to target the game. Spaniels are typically conveniently sized as pets, and they are quite popular because of that. The behaviors that Spaniels exhibit include cheerfulness, energy, and the love of fetching items. However, they also tend to display behaviors like possessiveness, destructiveness, or "rage syndrome." Rage syndrome is especially common in breeds like Cockers or Springers. The behavior is often characterized by attacking and biting, even with no provocation.

Breeds of Spaniels include: Clumber, Cocker, English Springer, Japanese Chin, Sussex, English Toy, and American Water

Companion dog type: Companion dogs are basically a mixed canine bag, with breeds ranging from Lhasa Apso to the Dalmatian. They typically don't fit in anywhere else. The poodle was originally a water hunting dog, the Tibetan Terrier and Lhasa Apso were guard dogs with herding abilities thrown into the mix, and the English Bulldog was a sporting dog. Behavior varies from breed to breed since companion dogs seem to come from all over the place. Typical problems that companion dogs may exhibit include the following: Dalmatians have a tendency to be aggressive towards other dogs and people, and they often need lots of exercise. The Boston terrier is known to be feisty and highly independent, the Schipperke is quite dominant, and often dominantly aggressive. Poodles often have separation anxiety and vocal issues.

Fighting dog type: Fighting dogs were bred to do what they are known for – fighting. Much of their aggression comes for their highly stimulated prey-drive, so it is not driven solely by their emotion. Thus, with tails wagging, fighting dogs actually appear to enjoy engaging in fights. Most of them are quite stubborn and independent. But they often display a trait that you may not expect – many are very affectionate and highly bonded with their owners, and the less erratic ones can make good dogs for children as well. Fighting dogs often display a wide variety of behaviors: Liveliness, affection, bond with owner, predatory instincts, and very focused most of the time. However, they can also display some problem behaviors, such as being untrustworthy with other dogs or animals, and occasionally showing aggressiveness towards humans.

Breeds of fighting dogs include the following: Sharpei, Bull Terrier, Pit Bull Terrier, Staffordshire, Staffordshire Bull Terrier, and Akita.

Pointer dog type: Pointers are good tempered, congenial dogs. They were originally bred to be hunting dogs. They are often large sized, and make good house pets so long as they get a sufficient amount of exercise due to their high energy levels. Pointers are often very intelligent, affectionate, clean, and loyal. Their aggression levels are almost non-existent, which makes them a perfect pet if you want them to co-exist amongst other dogs or animals. They are often very good with children and fit well with family life in general. Some typical problem behaviors they may exhibit are the tendency to run away, disobedience, and destructive behavior.

Breeds of pointer dogs include the following: German Shorthair, Irish, English, and Gordon Setters, and Wirehaired and English Pointers

Terrier dog type: Terriers are a subcategory of fighting dogs, so they exhibit much of the same characteristics. Terriers are known to be notoriously feisty with other dogs; they are bred to hunt solo and thus required little to no sociability. If socialized from a very early age, terriers could get used to being friendly with other dogs or humans. But even with appropriate amounts of socialization, terriers are best suited to be taken care of in single dog homes, and may not do well in public places like dog parks. Terriers were originally bred to chase down and kill small animals, which can make them a hazard to other pets, particularly cats and rodents. They will never be good candidates for a home with small animals since their predatory drive is high. However, they are commonly friendly towards their owners. They can also be quite dominant, and are deemed as poor pets for kids due to their tendency to bite.

Terrier dog breeds include the following: Boston, Border, Airedale, Australian, Bull, Tibetan, West Highland White, Wire Fox, Yorkshire, Lakeland, Norfolk, Scottish, Silky, and Welsh.

Hound dog type: Hound dogs are perhaps the oldest kind of hunting breeds. Two types of hound dogs exist – those who hunt by sight and those who hunt by scent. Sight hounds are rather sleek and speedy, while scent hounds are tough and reliable when you're off the road. Both types have been bred for centuries to master working independently, so they often have minds of their own and aren't the type of dog to respond to commands with no hesitation. Training hounds is a bit more difficult than training your typical dog, since many of them want to understand why you're asking them to do something rather than following orders blindly. If they don't believe that what you're doing is a good idea, then they're likely to ignore you and go on about their own business. All hounds will require a secure yard and walks on leash, especially sight hounds. Sight hounds will immediately take off after anything in motion, even if it takes them into a dangerous path of a car. Scent hounds will just wander off if they get a hold of an interesting scent.

Hound dog breeds include the following: Greyhound, Beagle, Bloodhound, Ibizan hound, Otterhound, Pharaoh hound, Plott, Saluki, and Harrier.

Northern dog breed: Northern dog breeds resemble wolves – they also often exhibit wolf-like behaviors. They are also used in breeding Wolf Hybrids. Northern dogs can be independent thinkers – they see themselves as a co-existent with you, not necessarily under you in the chain of command. As a result, Northern dog breeds can be hard to train because of their independence, but if you establish yourself as a firm and consistent leader, they will follow you. If you're not firm, they do have a tendency to walk over you. But beware! Firmness and consistency is critical, but do not use harsh training methods on Northern dog breeds. It will most likely backfire, and you can create an aggressive wolf-like being as a result. Typical problem behaviors that these dogs will exhibit are wandering, the urge to kill small animals, difficult to obedience train, and a strong dominant possessiveness.

Northern dog breeds include the following: Siberian Husky, Alaskan Malamute, American Eskimo, Norwegian Elkhound, American husky, and Samoyeds.

Toy dog breed: No, before you ask, they're not toys. They are dogs, considered to be "toy-like" due to their size. Most of these little guys have the breed characteristics of their larger cousins.

Due to their tiny nature, they can often be very snappy, no matter what breed they were bred from, and they can also develop their own behavioral problems, especially a dislike of being put on the ground. The smallest of toy dogs are considered to be "teacup dogs," though the terminology isn't accepted by all major dog registries. Toy dogs are a kind of companion animal – often slow moving, with little need for exercise and low endurance. However, they also display typical problem behaviors like snappiness, being very vocal, shy, exhibiting signs of separation anxiety, and dominant aggression.

Breeds of toy dogs include the following: Chihuahua, Italian Greyhound, Toy Poodle, Silky and Yorkshire Terriers, Pug, Japanese Chin, Affenpinscher, English Toy Spaniel, Pomeranian, Shih Tzu, and Maltese.

Chapter 1: The Initial Few Months – Common Problems and Their Solutions

The joy and excitement of bringing home a puppy is something that is difficult to put into words. If you have already have a puppy (which I'm assuming you do), then I am sure you understand what I mean. If you are still in the process of bringing home a little pup, then you will soon be able comprehend the meaning of the above statement. For you enthusiastic new owners, it would be nice if you kept your home equipped with some items that your dog will definitely need. The basic list includes:

A leash and collar – these are must have items. Until you train your dog, and until they are fully prepared to handle the outside world, you will definitely need to keep them on a leash in public.

Containment products like crates and a playpen; these are also important must have items. Until you have housetrained your dog, you will often need to keep them in a more confined space so that you can monitor and keep an eye out for them.

A comfortable dog bed is important in order to keep your beloved new friend as warm, cozy, and happy as possible until he or she is used to their new home. During the initial few days, your dog may be a little bit frightened of their new surroundings; small joys like the comfort of a warm bed will help them through this trying phase.

Food! Food is very critical, indeed. Small though he or she may be, your puppy is bound to have a large appetite, and you need to be prepared to feed that already large and steadily growing appetite. Moreover, just like babies, good nutrition is very important for the development of your dog's bones, skin, and organs.

Now that we have a list of the basic items you'll need out of the way, let's focus on some of the training aspects. This early-age stage of your dog's life is the optimal period for instilling them with basic disciplinary habits. Here are some of the most important practices that you must teach your dog:

Reward and punishment (positive and negative reinforcement). This is one of the most effective ways of training your puppy to know what behavior is acceptable and what is not. It is important to positively reinforce good behavior with something that your dog likes (i.e. treats); it is also important to punish bad behavior by alerting your dog to the fact that you are not happy with them (i.e. raising your voice). These reinforcements should occur immediately after the action. If you delay reinforcement, then your dog may think you are rewarding or punishing them for what they are doing in the current moment, as opposed to what they were doing before.

It is important to note that physically abusive punishment is never, ever acceptable. Rattling a can, blowing a horn, a stern 'no', and other such punishment techniques are more than enough to get you results. Moreover, ensure that these punishment techniques are not over performed, as you do not want your dog to associate the very act of punishment with you; this may cause your new family member to become afraid of you, and that is something that you don't want.

Last but not least, as you will learn, ignoring your dog is one of the best and most effective forms of punishment – it will work wonders for you, as your dog hates it when they feel as though you are upset with them…they will do anything to win your love back!

Rough play. This may be fun in the beginning, but if not controlled it can turn your dog into an unpopular one, especially with children and with those who fear dogs. The best way to control your dog's pawing, jumping, biting, and other physical games is to simply raise your voice. If that is not doing the trick, then try to ignore them and their behavior and walk away (pending they are not hurting or causing any imminent threat to anyone).

There are many times when dogs will pick up socks and other such items with their mouth and run around the house in hopes of getting your attention. These are acts of rough play used specifically by the canine to grab your attention. While it may seem cruel to ignore your new friend, especially since you also want to play with them, please remember that if you do not curb this rough-play attitude now, then correcting it later will be almost impossible. And you do not want a rowdy dog that you cannot even manage in your own house, right? Remember, you are doing this out of love for your dog – they will lead a better life because of it.

During these instances, either raising your voice or ignoring your dog and walking away in the opposite direction work very well, and they will soon get the message that such rough play is not allowed in your home.

Biting and destructive behavior. Puppies need to be taught to be gentle in their interactions with humans, and it's best to instill this in them when they are still young and able to learn. When your puppy is small, them biting your hand may not hurt. However, it is important to negatively reinforce this behavior when they are young. When your dog does bite, loudly shout out as if you are in pain and walk away from them. Soon, they will come to realize that biting you is a strict no-no. Your dog's teeth will become bigger, stronger, and sharper as he or she grows older. This can result in some serious damage done when they do bite, so it's crucial to teach them that it is wrong at a very early stage of their development.

Chewing is one of the acutely visible and annoying forms of destructive behavior that your little dog will likely exhibit. Keep an ample amount of items around that are O.K. for them to chew on, but make it very clear which items are allowed for chewing, and which are not. Until your dog completely understands this, do your best to keep an eye out for them.

Digging is a natural dog "activity," and if not controlled, it can reflect poorly in their behavior. Never let your dog go outdoors if you cannot monitor them. Digging is usually associated with a number of canine activities including, but not limited to, the act of digging out a chipmunk, squirrel, or some other rodent if they can smell one, digging to hide their bone, and digging because they are hot.

If you know the source of your dog's digging, or the reason why they are digging, then eliminate it in order to stop them for continuing. Get rid of that chipmunk from your garden, get your puppy a sand pit to hide their bone, and, perhaps, get your puppy a wading pool in order to help them cool off on hot summer days. You'll need to keep track of this and determine appropriate solutions.

Barking is another behavior that must be controlled. Do not leave your dog unattended in public places without having trained them to control their barking, as this can be a huge nuisance to your neighbors and others in your area. Simply saying "no barking" in a stern manner every time your dog barks will allow them to slowly realize that you are negatively reinforcing that behavior. But your persistent effort is needed in order to keep this raucous activity in check.

Try not to **shout** at your dog when he or she is barking; this will only ensure that the two of you would be barking together. Here are some effective ways to prevent or stop your dog from barking:

1) Eliminate the source of their barking. Your dog will often bark when they are fearful of something. Do your best to find the source of their fear, and work on removing it.

2) Ignore their barking. This method has worked brilliantly for dog owners over the years. Simply ignore your dog completely until he or she has stopped barking. By giving them attention, you are only enhancing their motivation to bark.

3) Get your dog accustomed to their barking sources. More often than not, your dog will bark when they see strangers, scurrying animals, children, etc. When training your dog, slowly get them used to these things, and gradually their barking will cease.

Handling hygienic activities. This includes bathing, trimming nails, cleaning ears, and other such procedures. These all require an early start so that when your dog becomes big, and hence more difficult to manage, they will already be used to these activities. They will put out their paws for nail trimming, prop up their ears so that you can clean them, and stand guard quietly while you bathe them.

Training a dog is a process that will provide everyone involved with so many benefits if it is started early enough. Do not hesitate to begin implementing the aforementioned tasks NOW – put your dog to work! Training your dog from an early age is a process that may seem trying at times, but it will significantly strengthen your bond and significantly increase the love, pride, and joy you feel for your new best friend.

Chapter 10
Training at Different Ages

Although a significant number of us consider our
canines relatives, closest companions, or reliable
associates, we view them as animals completely
not the same as ourselves. Indeed, they stroll on
4 legs and have a seriously unique understanding
of what tomfoolery is, but at the same time
they're actually similar to us here and there.
Learning, shockingly, is one of these ways.
Consider it. Numerous youngsters and youthful
grownups these days have grown up with a tablet
in their grasp. They saw how to utilize a tablet at
an early age, so presently all innovative advances
are simple things to dominate. They're actually
similar to a little dog being prepared in this
manner susceptible and profoundly responsive.
But does this mean that someone who**didn't**
grow up using a tablet can't use or master it? Of

course not. With training and differing levels of tolerance, anybody of all ages can figure out how to utilize a tablet, and even better, achieve complex undertakings utilizing one. A similar thought applies to more seasoned canines. Since they're more seasoned doesn't mean they can't learn new deceives. It simply implies they could require somewhat more practice time and you could should be somewhat more understanding while at the same time instructing them.

All this is to say, regardless of your pup or canine 's age, the person can be appropriately prepared and shown new orders and deceives. Certain limitations and difficulties can obviously spring up contingent upon your canine's genuineness and mental state, yet large numbers of these elements, as well, can be survived. And of course there **are** ideal times to train a dog. A common guideline of thumb is the more youthful, the better, however this totally doesn't mean you can't prepare your 10 year old German shepherd how to"talk," or your 12 year old Poodle how to"stay."

To help clarify some of these training-age misconceptions, I've included this helpful chapter that discusses age-specific techniques and restrictions of dog training. We'll take a specific look at training puppies and young dogs (6 weeks to 2 years old) and training older dogs (8 years to 12 years old).

Training Puppies and Young Dogs

For little dogs, the preparation general guideline is this: assuming your pup conscious, the individual can be prepared. Tragically, numerous accidental or unpracticed canine proprietors don't know about this, and that implies a few doggies go a long time prior to getting appropriate preparation. Moreover, there's a typical misinterpretation that recommends little dogs don't hold the data they're given or the information they learn until 3 or 4 months old. Notwithstanding, this simply isn't true. Canine reproducer after canine raiser have vouched that this is a simple fantasy hundreds have taken a stand in opposition to their encounters and accomplishment with preparing 4-multi week old doggies how to sit, remain, and come.

So assuming you wind up inviting a youthful, lively, 4-legged relative into your family, invest in some opportunity to peruse the accompanying data about age-explicit preparation for little dogs and youthful canines (once more, ages 6 weeks to 2 years old).

Training deadlines

Although pups and canines can learn new orders and deceives at whatever stage in life, starting preparation when you bring back your doggy is great. Most specialists suggest:

.Your puppy should be fully trained before **6 months old .**

Waiting until after your puppy is 6 months old makes training a slower and more challenging process because they've developed bad habits that have gone unpunished and uncorrected

Think about it: a multi month old doggy who has been permitted to run rampant
 around the house, biting on anything objects they can view inside mouth's span is going as objects be when directed. The multi month old pup has grown up realizing that this isn't alright; the half year old pup will be totally befuddled when you say their ways of behaving are no longer acceptable.

In Chapter 2 we gave a rundown of the 8 orders each doggy should know and at what age they ought to have dominated the orders by. You could find it supportive to survey these orders and age cutoff times assuming you've forgotten them.

Training restrictions

"Alright, my lord has a treat and advised me to sit, so presently I'm going toball."

Puppies are unimaginably moldable animal with regards to showing them what activities you like and what ways of behaving you hate. Notwithstanding, numerous pups are also:

- Highly energetic
- Have short attention spans
- Easily distracted

Multi-minded

The basic jingle of keys in the following room over can rapidly discourage a pup from their preparation and send them scrambling off to examine the especially intriguing sound. You'll should show restraint during this cycle. It's unavoidable

- you can't stick your doggy's feet to the ground to guarantee their full focus. Remember that you will experience difficulties while preparing a little dog, but that the challenges you face in the first 6 months of training will be relatively simple and temporary compared to the ones you'll encounter should you wait to train until your pup is 6 months or older.

Training Older Dogs

Although some myths do circulate among training puppies, the myths that exist among training older dogs are far greater. And that's just it— they're myths. Dogs are smart creatures, no matter their age. Sure, training an older dog may require a different training deadline and may have different restrictions than a puppy, but it's still an entirely feasible task. Older dogs are very much like older people: a senior citizen can learn how to use the latest technological gadget with the right amount of instruction, practice, and patience, just like an older dog can learn how to "speak" with the right amount of positive reinforcement, practice, and patience from the their instructor.

Training deadlines

Puppies have a proposed preparing cutoff time preferably, a doggy will be totally prepared by a half year old. Mature canines, then again, don't fall inside these edges. Preparing will truly rely upon every individual canine their own receptivity, their preparation history, their eagerness to learn, and their acumen. You will not have the option to set explicit cutoff times for when your canine will dominate a stunt,"Cushioned will figure out how to "dance" by next Tuesday," for instance yet you can set cutoff times that mark when you should stop your particular preparation assuming no outcomes approach"On the off chance that Fluffy doesn't dominate the"dance" order inside the following 2 months, we'll continue on." It'd be great to prompt you on a particular preparation cutoff time, yet that is just unrealistic with more established canines, sadly. All things being equal, you'll require to:

.

Gage: Determine what your dog's physical and mental abilities are.
Will my dog's arthritis prevent her from going up on her back legs and learning the "dance" command?

Judge: Think about how the training is going so far.
Is my dog showing progress, or are our efforts unproductive?

.

Adjust: Reflect on your success and determine if there's something you can adjust in order to increase productivity. ***What if I teach my dog to dance on all fours instead?***

Assess: At the end of each week, assess your dog's progress.

My dog shows signs of progression. She's completed the command once or twice. I'll give it another month before reassessing again.

Training restrictions

The limitations that will more often than not accompany preparing more seasoned canines are what presumably fills the talking about, "you can't impart new habits when old ones are so deeply ingrained." But stop and think for a minute: this maxim incorporates every single more established canine. Notwithstanding, there are a lot of more seasoned canines that impeccably learn new orders in practically no time. For the canines that battle, it's not on the grounds that they're not savvy. This is on the grounds that they have mental or actual limitations that keep them from finishing orders. The absolute most normal motivations behind why more seasoned canines face preparing limitations are:

.Arthritis: Many older dogs will experience various forms of arthritis. Some dogs can carry on with daily physical activities without much effort, while others struggle to walk. Commands such as "dance," "roll over," "play dead," and "paw" might not be an option depending on your dog's arthritis location and progression, but commands like "stay," "lay down," "sit," "leave it," and "speak" might still be viable options.

.Canine Cognitive Disorder: This disorder, more commonly known as "Doggie Alzheimer's" alters your dog's mental state. Frequent disorientation, decreased hearing, restlessness, and decreased desires for physical activities can make it challenging to train your dog.

There are different limitations that you 'll need to think about while preparing your
 more established canine. Remember, nonetheless, that psychological circumstances, particularly, aren't truly seen all of the time. You might become disappointed following 3 months when your canine actually hasn't figured out how to "talk," yet their powerlessness could originate from mental issues. Along these lines, we firmly suggest that you:

.Talk to your vet before you begin training. Your vet will be able to provide a full mental and physical work-up of your dog so that you know *beforehand* what commands or tricks won't be received or physically capable by your dog.

Training Tips for Dogs of All Ages
Whatever your doggy or canine's age might be,

it's vital that you approach preparing with these thoughts in mind:

.**Positivity.** Your puppy or dog needs to be a willing participant when it comes to learning new commands and tricks. Training isn't just about the owner—it's an interaction that requires motivation and willingness on **both** sides.

Patience. A puppy is **going** to get distracted during training. There's no doubt about this. You'll need to be patient while you train them— learn what times of day they learn the best and take advantage of it. Likewise, an older dog **will** struggle to understand a new command when it's one that demands them to break a habit they've been allowed to do for years. Again, patience is crucial here—put yourself in your dog's shoes. Imagine what it would be like if someone told you to stop doing something you've been doing all your life.

chapter 11

Keeping A Pet Bugg Dog

The Bugg dog, a cross between the Boston Terrier and the Pug, is an excellent family pet because of its endearing and cuddly nature. Due to its adorable look and upbeat personality, The Bugg is sure to win over every family member.

This hybrid breed inherits the best traits from its two parent breeds. Bugg dogs are great friends for both children and adults because of their friendly and outgoing attitude. Whether it's a little apartment or a large house, they are highly adaptable and perform well in a variety of living settings.

In general, buggs are easy to train and eager to please their owners. They like taking frequent walks and playing with others since they don't have a lot of energy. Due to their sturdy design and modest size, they are ideal for families with limited room.

Additionally, Bugg's short coat requires minimal maintenance, making it useful for households with busy schedules. They are normally healthy canines with minimal breed-specific health issues.

In conclusion, anybody who is lucky enough to own a Bugg dog as a pet will find it to be a fantastic addition to their family, providing them with joy, love, and endless entertainment.

Environment And Living Situations For Bugg Dog

The beautiful and tiny Bugg dog, commonly referred to as a Boston Terrier and Pug cross, combines the greatest traits of both of its parent breeds. The Bugg dog is adaptable and can thrive in a range of home settings and living conditions.

Bugg dogs are perfect for apartment living because of their little height. They don't need a large yard, but regular walks and games will help to keep their brains and bodies busy. A Bugg dog may find that regular inside fun and brief outside excursions fulfill his need for activity.

With regard to their living conditions, Bugg dogs often exhibit versatility and function well in a range of situations. They are believed to be social and like hanging out with their human relatives. So it's important to make sure youngsters interact with people often and aren't left alone for long periods. Bugg dogs could also enjoy having a comfortable and homey space, such as a dog bed or specific area where they can relax and take a break.

It's crucial to puppy-proof the home, remove any potential hazards, and provide the Bugg dogs with appropriate chew toys to give them a safe environment.

In conclusion, as long as Bugg dogs have adequate exercise, have chances for social interaction, and reside in a safe and pleasant environment, they may thrive in a variety of living arrangements, including apartments.

As A Working Dog, Bugg Dog

The Boston Terrier and Pug hybrid breed known as the Bugg dog has a special blend of characteristics that make it an effective working dog. The Bugg performs well in a variety of activities because of its intelligence, agility, and high work ethic, despite not being historically known as a working breed.

The great intellect of Bugg dogs, despite their little size, makes them fast learners and trainable. They are good candidates for obedience training and duties requiring cerebral stimulation since they are noted for being attentive and eager to please their owners.

The Bugg can carry out a variety of job duties because of its agility and muscular stamina. For instance, their small stature and agility enable them to perform jobs like search and rescue in confined locations effectively. They are useful in circumstances where bigger canines cannot access them because of their ability to maneuver through tight spaces and tiny gaps.

Additionally, they communicate well with humans because of their amiable and gregarious natures, which is a crucial quality for therapy or support dogs. To those in need, Buggs may provide emotional support, solace, and company.

Though less well-known than other working breeds, the Bugg dog excels in a variety of jobs because of its intelligence, agility, and adaptability. The passion, energy, and dependability they may offer to any work at hand should not be undervalued despite their little stature.

Breeding And Procreation Of The Bugg Dog

The Boston Terrier and Pug were the parents of the lovely crossbreed known as the Bugg dog, also known as the Boston Terrier Pug hybrid. It is crucial to take into account the traits and health factors of both parent breeds while breeding and reproducing Bugg dogs.

To produce Bugg dogs, a purebred Boston Terrier and a purebred Pug are intentionally mated. The objective is to have a litter of pups that combines the best qualities of both breeds. Breeders that practice responsible breeding make sure that both parents are fit, free from hereditary diseases, and have had the necessary health exams.

For Bugg dogs, the reproductive process follows a predictable pattern. About twice a year, female Bugg dogs go into estrus or heat. They can conceive during this period because they are fertile. On the other hand, male Bugg dogs mature sexually between the ages of six and eight months. When both the male and the female are in prime reproductive condition, breeding normally takes place.

The female Bugg dog goes through a gestation period of around 63 days after a successful mating. She will go through physical and hormonal changes during this period. To guarantee the health of the pregnant mother and the growing pups, it is essential to offer the right care, diet, and veterinary assistance.

The Bugg dog will give birth to a litter of pups after the gestation time is through. There may be variations in typical litter size, which may range from three to six pups. Both of the parent breeds' characteristics will be passed down to the pups, who will need appropriate socialization, education, and medical care as they mature.

To generate pups with favorable features, Boston Terriers and Pugs are intentionally mated in the breeding process and reproduction of Bugg dogs. Responsible breeders give both parent dogs' health and well-being priority and take the appropriate precautions before, during, and after giving birth.

Chapter 12

How to Make your Puppy Accept Handling?

Similar to individuals, canines can likewise be watchful or restless when they are taken care of by individuals they don't have the foggiest idea. At times, these fuzzy creatures will get unnerved when their proprietors contact or nestle them.

Living with a canine that you can 't play, embrace or contact is without a doubt something miserable. Entirely comparable with a relationship has lost its flash. The motivation behind why this happens is that doggies have changing insights with regards to contacting or different types of taking care of. At the point when they are being embraced by somebody they know, they will generally be easygoing and quiet. Nonetheless, when an outsider does likewise activity, they become forceful. This will in general be a major issue while going to the vet or groomer.

For outrageous circumstances, wild canines should have been sedated before the custodian can trim their hair. That is the reason you want to help your little dog to turn out to be more friendly, even to strangers.

Make your Family Members Hug your Puppy

With management, permit your children to pat and embrace your pet. Assuming that you have visitors, make them join the action. Continue doing this sort of preparing until he figures out how to be loose around other people.

people.

 month old young adult dog is now challenging to deal with, so it's ideal to begin early

Try Other Forms of Physical Handling

Once your puppy turns out to be more acclimated with embracing, have a go at getting him and putting him on your lap for a long time. You can likewise rub his paunch or give him a kiss on the nose.

What to Do When your Pooch Resists?

During the initial not many times, don 't expect that your pet will effectively warm up to your other relatives or visitors. On the off chance that he pitches a fit, don't relinquish him without any problem. Assuming you surrender to his brutal battle, your little guy might feel that he can have a tantrum whenever he wants.

To keep him in a meek position, hold his collar with one hand and put the other on his back. Make him rests on your mid-region and tenderly hold him until he quiets down. Rub his ear and paunch to relieve him. In the event that your dog

quiets down, acclaim him and let him go.

Chapter 13

Understanding Barking, Whining and Biting

One of the manners in which canines speak with different canines and people is through vocal sound like barks and cries. Each sort of canine vocal sounds has various implications. To figure out what they truly need to say, you additionally need to consider their non-verbal communication and current mood.

Barking

There are a few motivations behind why canines bark. They might have a compromised outlook on something, they need to caution their pack, they are exhausted or restless, or they simply need to play with you.

If your canine is bothered or he is experiencing fearing abandonment, his barks might will more

often than not be piercing. The pitch of his bark
goes higher the more he becomes upset.

 If your canine is simply woofing on the grounds
that he's exhausted, it will have a tedious and dull
sound.
 However, assuming you hear a bark that has a
sharp tone, it implies that your pet is cautioning
you about something.

Demand barks, then again, are additionally sharp.
Nonetheless, they can likewise be tenacious and
are normally focused on the human who
furnishes the canine with all his needs.

If you have any desire to keep your canine from
yapping unreasonably, ensure that you have a
steady reaction to it. If you find his barking
unacceptable, use a command phrase such as
"stop barking". Nonetheless, on the off chance
that he barks to alarm you about something,
acclaim him or give him a treat.

Whining

This kind of canine vocalization is shrill and is made nasally while the canine's mouth is shut. Canines cry when they need something or when they need to play outside. This is additionally used to communicate frustration.

When your little dog whimpers, try not to comfort him a lot of on the grounds that he might feel that you are lauding his way of behaving. However much as could reasonably be expected, disregard your pup when he is crying. This will cause him to understand that he can't get your endorsement when he whines too much.

Biting

While your fuzzy buddy is as yet youthful, you must address his gnawing conduct so you won't encounter any challenges in the future.

You want to further develop his chomp hindrance, or the capacity to change the power of his nibble. Pups with powerless nibble hindrance will more often than not chomp harder on the grounds that they don't have the foggiest idea how delicate the human skin can be.

If you own few doggies, they can without much of a stretch further develop their chomp restraint by playing. Notwithstanding, in the event that you only one, don't stress since you can in any case improve it.

To do this, simply play with your pup and permit him to nip your hands. Assuming he unexpectedly nibbles, cry and imagine that you are harmed. This will prevent him from gnawing your hand.

 What's more, give him a bite toy to get his teeth far from human skin.

Chapter 14

Bathing and Grooming

What to remember

Before actually grooming your dog, you have to understand that you also have to tie positive association with giving the dog a bath. For example, instead of scaring by forcing him when it's time for a bath, you should use a clear and calm voice and gently coax him.

This also means that after a bath, you should go ahead and praise him, and give him treats. This way, he will see grooming time as a fun experience—and it will be easier to get him to take a bath next time!

Start Them Young

Another important thing to keep in mind is that it would be best to start the habit of bathing and grooming a dog early. See, puppies find it hard to oppose to whatever it is that you want them to do, which means it'll be easier for them to adapt the behavior overtime.

Protect the Ears

Also, make sure that you protect your puppy's ears. Take care when rinsing him and don't spray water directly into them. Now, let's get to grooming your dog!

Bathing the Dog

According to the ***American Kennel Club***, you can bathe a dog every three months or so. However, during summer, or when the weather is too hot, it would also be okay to bathe your dog more frequently.

Here's a good bath time routine:

Remove dead hair and mats by brushing the dog's hair.

To secure footing, place a rubber mat in the bathtub and fill it up with around 3 to 4 inches of lukewarm water.

Wet the dog thoroughly by using a spray hose, but make sure not to directly spray the ears, eyes, and nose.

Massage the dog's coat with shampoo, specifically made for dogs—and do it from head to tail.

Use a pitcher or a spray hose for rinsing.

Check if there is any debris or foul odors in the ears, and use cotton ball for shallow cleansing, but please make sure not to hit the ear canal.

Use a large towel and blow dryer to dry your pet after. If you're going to use a blow dryer, make sure to monitor the level of heat. Remember how you would like it if someone were forcing air that is too hot on your head.

Brushing Hair

As mentioned earlier, it is important to brush a dog's coat to spread natural oils and keep it silky smooth. Doing so will also prevent debris from forming, and help keep his skin irritant-free. It also keeps him safe from fleas, and other allergens.

As you may know by now, dogs have different kinds of coats. Here's what you have to do for each of them.

Short and Smooth Coat

Loosen dirt and dead skin by using rubber brush.

Remove dead hair by using bristle brush.

And finally, use a chamois cloth to polish the dog's hair!

Dense and Short Fur

Remove tangles by using a slick brush.

Use bristle brush to catch dead hair.

Comb the tail!

Luxurious and Long Coat

1. For this one, you have to be patient as you'd have to remove tangles   every day.

Use a slicker brush and then gently tease out his mats.

And finally, use a bristle brush to polish his coat.

Clipping the Nails

You need lots of patience when it comes to clipping a dog's nails, because most dogs get a little upset about this. Not only are dogs uncomfortable with their paws being handles, but unlike human nails, they have nerves and blood veins in their nails. So it is very important you are careful with this step. What you have to do now is make sure that you prepare your dog for handling of his paws.

To do so, massage your dog's feet so that he would be used to the feeling of someone holding and rubbing his feet. Press down each toe, and don't forget to give him treats as you do so. Now, on to clipping:

Inspect if there is any dirt or debris by spreading each of your dog's feet.

Cut off the tip of each nail with guillotine-type clippers as they are the sharpest. Start just before the nail begins to curve.

Avoid the vein that runs into the nail (this is called "quick"). If you are unsure where the quick begins, ask your vet to help you find it. If you accidentally cut the quick too many times, there is a good chance your dog will shy away from nail clipping altogether, since it will be painful for him.

If you accidentally cut "quick", just make sure to apply styptic powder on the affected area.

Use emery board to smoothen edges out.

Keep these tips in mind and your dog would always be happy and clean!

Other Obedience Training Commands: Fetch, Shake Paw, and Roll Over

Although the above are the main obedience training commands, you can also teach your dog the following additional obedience training commands:

How to Teach the Shake Paw Command

Suppose your dog likes jumping on unfamiliar people he comes across. The shake paw command can stop this risky behavior and make your dog admirable to visitors.

Here is see how to teach your dog to shake paws:

Place your dog in the sit command; once he is in a seated position, firmly enclose a delicious treat in your hand and ensure your dog smells but does not see or access the treat.

Bring your enclosed treat hand near the dog's nose sideways until your dog's head slightly turns towards you.

Encourage the dog to reach for the treat; the dog will try to open your closed hand using his paws.

Once his paw touches your hand, open the hand and allow him to have the delicious treat.

Praise him and repeat the exercise a couple of times alternating from one side to the other. Ensure your dog uses the right paw each time.

Add a command before you give the reward; for instance you can say, "How's my dog" then award the treat.

Hold out the other hand that does not have the

treat in an open position. When the dog touches

the open hand, say the command and reward

him. Repeat this new exercise a number of times

with both paws.